Table for two Please

WRITTEN BY **RODNEY TUCKER**

THE SECRET ART GALLERY | ILLUSTRATED BY LEERON MORRAES

Beansprout Books LLC | Morongo Valley, California

love poems by
RODNEY TUCKER

Table for two Please

ISBN: 978-1-950471-10-2
ISBN-10: 1-950471-10-1

No part of this book may be reproduced or transmitted in any form or by any means, electronic or mechanical, including photocopying, recording, or by any information storage or retrieval system, without permission in writing from the publisher.

Library of Congress Control Number: 2019948656

www.beansproutbooks.com

Morongo Valley, California

2019

SEASONS

I can't believe she's going to leave me.
I couldn't help not to fall
after all
Summer came and went so fast,
something in me knew she wouldn't last
As hot as she was,
I'm just thankful things are cooling down.
Her dress was soft and white like a fresh layer of snow
Icy eyes...
smooth with a nice glow,
I call her Wynter
I tried to fight it then it all made sense.
Spring's my favorite season I'm convinced.

MONA LISA ROSE

Peace, Life, and Energy.
Attitude with class. Simplistic lifestyle with pizazz.
Slim thick body
Sounds like a wife for your ass.
Of course.
that's just a few of thousands of thoughts when I think of you...
YOU! YES YOU!
The woman I can smile about when I'm feeling blue.
Lie detector tests say I'm true to you.
Social media search history probably prove it boo.
Another sleepless night mind consumed with you.
Wanting to text you baby it's true!
I been fighting but I feel that I'm in love with you.
Baby.. Everything between us just happened so naturally.
I remember wondering if we would kiss.
Electrifyingly satisfying.
Is my classification of our exchange in energy.
All I had to do was be patient and see.
You put me inside your bubble and around you I could feel no pain.
From 281 to my city.
I'll scream your name!
A vicious cycle if you will.
Here we are and there you go, overcome my body with chills.

Reminiscing on past times, hoping you will.
I get sad and fall into a sunken place.
If only I could get out.
Stomach nervous like I can't get the words out.
Standing before you with a heart full of words.
While my heart beats loudly like a stampeding herd.
Excuse this awkward moment but I can't help to stare.
Maybe I need some teal.
To help me get things moving.
My very own Mona Lisa.
With the coldest features in the warmest climate.
Take it back to 2k13 when you told me to get behind it.
Can we rewind it?
How could you make me feel so good when life was tough?
I just want to hold and kiss you I promise that's enough!
All my memories, everything about you is pure.
At a period of life where I don't know much,
but when I think about you I'm sure.
But what if it was just me.
Hopelessly battling the storm while lost at sea.
Or maybe I just need some T.
Some quality time with you I feel that it will do.
Mona Lisa Rose...
I love you more than the picture I paint for you to see.

MONA LISA ROSE

KARAOKE

Bright lights set a small stage -- melanin...
laughs and drinks let's get carried away!
Brown eyes!
Yes you, I enjoy your stare.
Sweet flower.
So soft, so sensitive, so mesmerizing.
I enjoy your hair!
Please do me the honor, as I hope to share...
a piece of you...
Your energy is pure...
I can't imagine being satisfied with just a piece of you.
Sweet flower, sing to me.
Tell me all the times they forgot to water you.
See, I know how it feels to be strained--
utilized for a greater purpose, respectfully
But, I also know how it feels to be drained--
left empty and inoperable.
Allow me, sweet flower...
Allow me to water your roots.
I see the beauty in your spirit sweet flower,
allow me to tell you the truth.

Passion lies behind those eyes.
I'd die and a kiss from you could revive me a thousand times.
I choose my words wisely the way that I choose my friends
In life I've learned when to go out
but more importantly when to stay in.
You appeal to my senses.
I can feel them tingling.
Shame on you for awakening my sensibility, unintentionally.
Fire, desire, and intensity...
I will serve you up.
By the time you realize you're close to empty
I'm already refilling your cup.
That's what happens when you're around people
that God sent you to see.
Lose yourself in your dreams, in your passions
no matter how weird or scary they might seem!
Weird is cool and weird is you,
embrace the moment and respect the truths.

                                        With Love

ALONE

Table for two please.
Thoughts crashing against my eardrums like waves in the night
Footsteps creeping in the background,
like bystanders around a turbulent fight.
Is anyone there?
Foolishly, I inquire inside my mind,
No words spoken yet my actions are screaming, mime.
Seconds, minutes, hours, any duration of time.
I want to get lost --
Lost like the favorite shirt you'll probably never find.
Contradicting, right?
Imagine the voices in my head.
Love being alone, yet I seek to be nurtured instead.
Am I afraid?
Afraid that you will know the real me and run far, far away.
Or am I afraid?
Afraid that you will know the real me and never, ever stray.
Feels like I'm rolling the dice...
Feels like I'm paying the price...
Happiness is grandma's apple pie,
but nobody saved me a slice.

I want to be bothered,
and alone in the same moment.
Am I crazy?
Is there something wrong with my mind?
I'll take the time to gather the pieces,
only to leave them all behind.
How do you have 20/20 vision,
yet to the world you are so blind?
Do you not understand your presence?
And how you can be so kind?
I want to be alone,
yet I want people to love me too.
Why can I feel so happy but still show my attitude?
There's something wrong with me.
I knew it all along.
Even in utter silence,
my mind constantly plays this song.
"Somehow even when no one is with me I'm never truly alone."
Somewhere down the line, this became my favorite song.

MYSTERIOUS GIRL

You
You're such a mystery
Smooth talking, angelic-walking, beautiful, beautiful girl
Spirit of a gypsy
So carefree and desirable
I'm drunk off your hustle, tipsy.
From afar you rock my world girl!
Lover of fine things like yourself
Creator of distinct vibes
Master of all tribes
Body of an ebony mermaid
Can I keep you for myself?
I promise to display you in my room of trophies...
not on a shelf but as a shrine.
I don't really know you yet
Yet you blow my mind
Naturalist
Enthusiast
Connoisseur of Earth's wonderful treasures
If I had to guess your measurements
PERFECT would seem clever
Your roots are so genuinely divine.
Curl pattern works just fine for me.

Not a flaw that any naked eye could see.
So then I ask, what does it take to be?
Free!
I can sense it in your conversation.
Free as the wind that may never strike my skin again.
Free as the rain that will dissipate into the atmosphere,
no longer stroking my window pane.
Free as the world pretends to be.
Free as you being you and me being me.
I long for your affection...
to be admired, inspired, dare I walk in your direction?
From the evils within you encompass your own protection.
Love falls short, yet you are love.
Pure as an all-white dove
Simultaneously sincere and harmonious as the heavens above.
I enjoy the thoughts that arise.
You take me higher without needing to climb.
A perfect poem on silky paper.
Never needing to rhyme.
I imagine you showing up late but being right on time.
You are the present.
You are the future.

What suits you?
What makes you tick?
I can't fathom you being hypnotized by tricks.
Simplistic manifestation of all things raw.
Raw feelings, raw materials
From the crown of your head down to the soles of your feet...
You are a Queen.
You are Complete.
Some energies need help to transfer
But you are my favorite cancer.
How can it be?
I found myself lost in sauce that was never made for me.
The mere thought of you gets my heart racing.
Complacent I could never be, out of fear of disappointing you.
You.
Beautiful, Beautiful you.
You are a mystery.
You intrigue every fiber of my being.
My words, my feelings, my actions...
My love for you is true!

                                    With Love

PRESENCE

Pain is seeing your bright smile illuminated in my absence.
I had you!
You were mine
Time didn't rewind and the future couldn't accept presents.
So it's all past tense.
How dare I feel a way when a man stepped up to the plate?
When all I ever did was stand in the dugout and wait.
I couldn't believe that just being present was enough.
Wishing I could fast-forward to the future
Because the present doesn't look too bright.
Hopeful, prayerful, I should be ashamed.
Hard to distinguish your voice with so many calling my name.
Truthfully
Genuinely
I never entertained the thought.
We were friends first
So a relationship I never sought.
One thing about life though
She will point out those mistakes
I yearn for you daily
Please don't tell me I'm too late.

We don't choose love but we can choose, love.
I'm sorry it took so long
I'm beginning to think that these feelings are far too strong.
And when I think I'm closer to you, I feel you moving on.
But wait
Is there a glimmer of hope for the union?
Please
Instruct me as you please!
I'll do whatever it takes to confront you with this knee.
I hold back so much pain
A freed mind is one that never presses rewind
Because the beauty is in the presence.
Somehow
Someway
I've got to gain some leverage.
Speak to me oh gentile spirit and guide me along the way.
Ignoring all the roadblocks and fences in our way...
Everything I've been through
It's starting to make perfect sense.
If only
Only if

                                    I could get out of the past tense.

I'M SORRY

Pain runs deeper than you catching him cheating
  texting
        snapping
                Instagramming-deleting
Deceit.
That damn deceit---
You mean to tell me out of all people you could fuck over
You choose to fuck over me?!
I'm impatient
I'm attitudinal
I'm disrespectful!
ME?!
I'm inconsiderate
I'm selfish
I'm intolerable!
ME?!
Pain runs deeper than finally dropping down to one knee
Ignoring her signals
You still ask and her
answer is "No..."

Transgression
So easily I approach
Attached to physical beauty masked over savagery.
It is her who is to blame young sir.

Or maybe dually so
You created an environment where misbehavior was acceptable.

Who are you to want to change?

Who are you to stay the same?

Pain runs deeper than the rejection of your Mother.
For some reason or another she acts as if I had a choice!
Thank God for angels to love and nurture my spirit.
My Mom needs help but she never could get it.

Help starts with you
Are you honestly doing all that you can do?
Success begins and ends with you
If you put in the work results will come too
Pain runs deeper than not getting a promotion, raise
an honorable mention and Chuckee Cheese Tokens

Reciprocity

The work I put in does not provide any satisfaction to me.

Financially, mentally, physically.

There's nothing to see!

"Have you....?"

"No I haven't.... It's not me!!"

Deep stares in the mirror are bound to reveal.

The love or hate you have and what's real.

Pain runs deeper than eviction notices
and honey bun birthday cakes.

This one I know most can't begin to relate.

In saying that it's love-always never hate.

But this pain is generational-deep and not for the faint.

Oppressed man, oppressed man yea that's me!!

I'M SORRY

Needy Love

I'll admit.
I require a lot of attention.
I want to not only be loved but feel loved.
What is it to know the glove is there?
If you can't feel it when the knife cuts?
Finding true love in you was the right touch.
The right touch I needed in my life.
To open my eyes and fight.
But I'm sick of fighting.
Feel like I've been doing that my whole life.
Fighting to be understood.
Appreciated and worthy.
I always wanted to feel love.
Like two white doves flying in unison.
I wanted to feel love like tight hugs at a loved ones' funeral.
I wanted to feel love like I never felt it before.
Like losing my phone on a boat trip
Yet it washes up to shore.

Your love is the **REAL** love.
No glove yet I yearn to feel every cut and still love.
The love I never knew I needed but damn sure needed love.

SO...

Rub on my head when you feel love, your touch is euphoric

I know it when we feel love.

Everything's a playground, can we run around like kids love?

See-saw and swings are such a thrill, but--

At times I feel empty...

and knowing that with a slight gesture

or calm words you can refill me.

They say check on your strongest friend.

I'm hurting and don't know where to begin.

You should see my eyes blink love.

Rapidly, so I don't let the fears sink love.

I'm damaged.

Even after all these years love.

I can't manage to clear my mind of it all.

But I'm in love with the fact that you bring me out of my shell.

All I know, everywhere I go in my mind

There you are.

My arms are reaching out to you but you're so damn far.

It's not a constant feeling

But when the pressure is on there is no ceiling.

I need to feel love.

That real love.

That I'm going to rub on his head just because kind of love.

That let me tell you about my plans for our kids love.

I need that baby I'm here love.

And I think what hurts so deep is that it's there.

But you pick and choose when to display it.
Every night since Saturday

I've had nightmares and I can't take it.
Dreams of you ignoring me for the next dude.
Dreams of you walking past me like some random fool.

I can't handle not feeling your love.
Even when I see the two doves, in unison.
It hurts too much.

I get this tight clinching in my gut.
FUCK!
I remember my first thoughts and reaction of being stuck.

Stuck loving you because your love is true.
But now when you take a day off I wonder who.
What, how, why, and when?

I can't handle the thought of not being with you
But more so not feeling the love you produce.

For I know the love you give is from God above
below
and all-around.

Your love is loud, although you don't hear a sound.

Sometimes I look sad and my face may offer a frown.

I promise you an ounce of your love will turn that upside down.

I try to contain my emotions and feelings.

I try to avoid being the villain.

In my eyes nobody can love like you do.
If I could quantify it
It would be infinity…

And now that I'm thinking of it

I know that's what gets me.

No matter how much of your love is in me
No matter how much others envy.

I need your love the same each day.
I need your love more than I need to pray.
Your love loves me and ensures I'm ok.

If it wasn't for your love who knows where my heart would be today.

I HAVE...

As the lights brightened
I realized how dark the room was becoming.
It was almost a perfect mixture of being confident and confused.
I allowed evil to inspire me--and somehow became her muse.
You can tell I can see but if you look closer you can see,
The look in my eyes, darkness...it did something to me.
Have you ever woken up early at the same time as the sun?
Blinking profusely, knowing the pain has just begun!
Sunshine creeping and I'm wide awake.
But I'd rather keep sleeping because I'm safer that way.
You can tell I can see but if you look closer you can see,
The look in my eyes, darkness... it did something to me.
Have you ever joined a room full of friends?
Happiness with erupting laughter,
but darkness persuaded you to pretend.
Not because you don't like these people, not because you're sad.
Because every time you try to smile the darkness shows her ass
Some will even ask, "Are you ok?"
Crazy thing about the darkness, you really feel that way.
So instead of sharing what's really on your mind...
You laugh and smile and fake it...hoping to leave her behind.
You can tell I can see but if you look closer you can see,
The look in my eyes, darkness... it did something to me.
Have you ever tried to escape?
Have you ever wanted to run far-far away?
Crazy no matter how fast or how far, the darkness seems to stay.

Time

Love it-Hate it.
Past, present, future.
Time.

Falling deeply for you.
Knowing I can't have you.
Silky long hair, with that tiny pretty face.
Come here let me grab you.
Lips soft like marshmallows, sweet enough to keep me drooling.
Eyes big, wide and bright, passionately school me.
Open up and let me in -- but please never try to fool me.

Time.

Embrace it-Endure it.
Present, future.

Time.

Is it you?
An opportunity to get closer... a dream come true!
Smooth skin with a radiant glow,
Fine as ever I want you to know,
Now that we're grown I can put on a show,
Pleasure runs deep I hear you reap what you sow..
Baby... of you I have so many thoughts and wishes.

Starting with a friendly hug that turns into fiery kissing,
Folding your clothes and washing the dishes,
Even if I can't stay for long you will feel my existence.
I want to make you dinner and run you a bath.
Massage your body and make you laugh,
My effort is endless you don't know the half.
I'm all about giving and gladly take last,
I want to paint you a picture and pray that it lasts..
My stroke is efficient like painting on glass..

Time.

Cherish it-Remember it

Future.

Come here and allow me to awaken your soul.
Where you are broken I can heal and make whole.
You're the kind of spirit that I could never let go.
I sense that you're delicate I need to go slow,
Extended hands, asking if you want to go..
Let's go get lost into

                                                        Time.

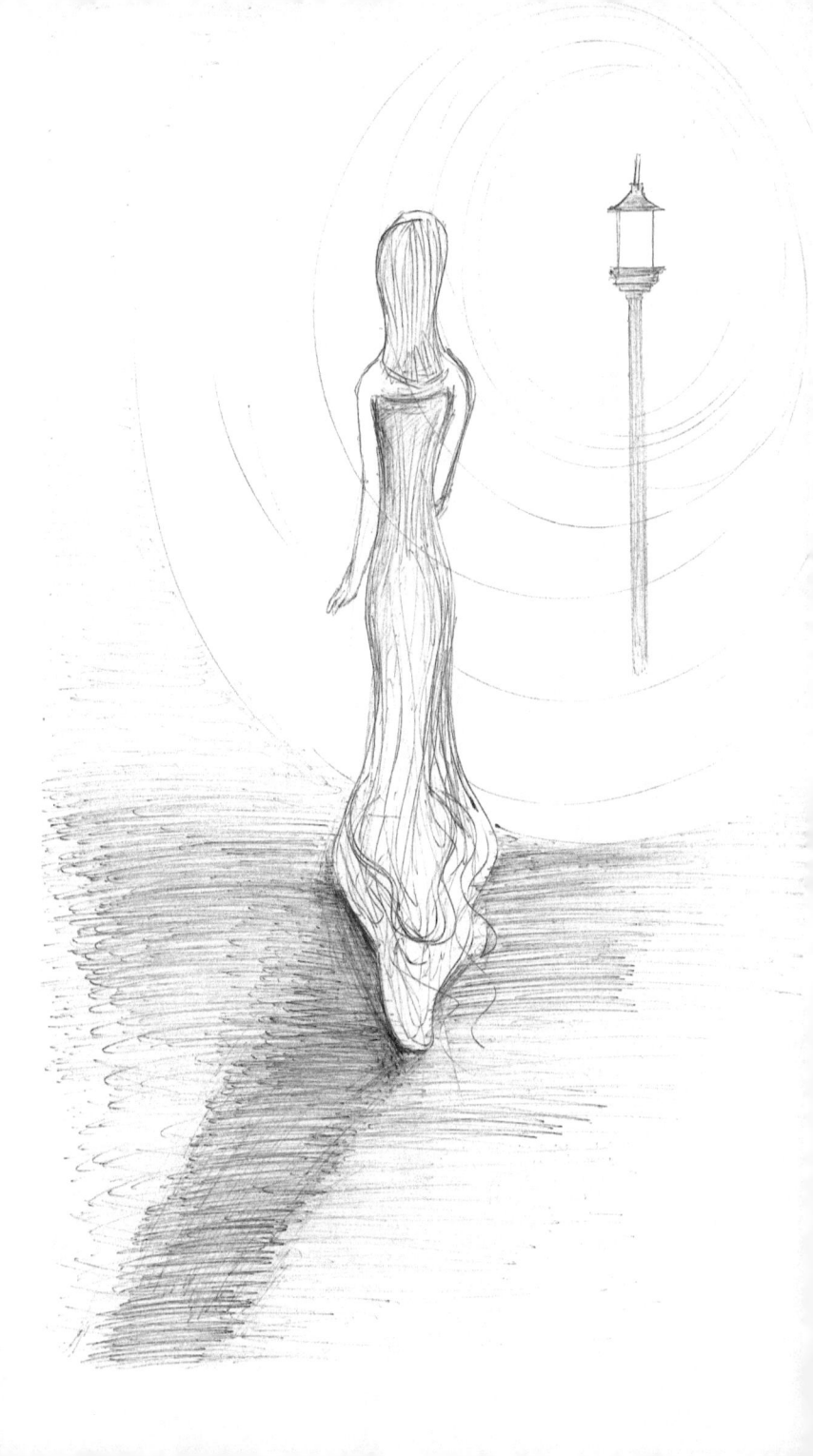

Muted

Sunrise... Sunset... Passion...
Elegant like a skyline, so beautiful and everlasting.
Moonlight, starlight, is it even light at all?
Desire burning in your eyes girl, why would I let you fall?
I like you, because like me, you do what you want
I can't even imagine you not doing what you want
Watching words drip from your juicy lips is so appeasing,
I like my tamales hot and you like teasing.
So easy it would be to try...
To close my eyes and take a bite, mmhmm, delightful!
But I see the deeper side, behind that big cerebral.
Gifted like Christmas morning with a divine spirit
Capable of warming cathedrals
See I... like you, can allow my words to be lethal.
No weapon formed against me shall prosper
Except my own tongue.
To someone, anyone, your words are the starting gun. BANG!
The racers take off, but not every one.
There's one who has learned to keep her pace.
She also used to expel all her energy,
at the beginning of the race.
Through experience and heartache, she's learned the ways.
I ask that you simply don't let passion fade.
Fade like the haircut, with the waves sitting deep.
Girl you're a leader, don't you follow those sheep!
Muted

Love Me! Or Leave Me Alone

The title speaks for itself, 'Love Me! Or Leave Me Alone.' I want you to get used to reading this because I want you to feel it. I want you to feel it at work when your co-worker now suddenly has an interest to speak to you after ignoring and looking right through you all week. I want you to feel it in your friendships and relationships in which you're able to somehow constantly convince yourself that the love is there, but is it really? I really want you to take a deep look at yourself and determine the type of love and energy you deserve. If those friendships or relationships or companionships or whatever ship aren't working, tell them "Love Me! Or Leave Me Alone."

I love everybody, even the people who don't love me back… Love isn't about being loved back. It's about loving unconditionally no matter what happens on the other end. A genuine spirit is God-sent, and the beauty of her love is in her vulnerability. The ability to be let down, to be hurt, to be disappointed. Remember this, love does NOT hurt people, people hurt people. That heartbreak from back in the day had nothing to do with love. Neither do the many marriages that fail. We're always so quick to blame love without realizing how ignorant we sound. Here you are blaming love for your failed relationship, but you can't even get ten people to share a similar interpretation of love. I can't tell you who-what-when-where-why or how to love, no one can, but I can instruct you on how to love me. My life is precious so either love me genuinely or leave me alone.

By now I'm sure many of you are saying, "Wait a minute dude, first you say 'Love Me! Or Leave Me Alone,' then you turn right around and say I love everybody, even the people who don't love me back...pick a side!" Well, my side is love. Solid, genuine, divine love. If I cannot giveth that love. I will not fake love you, I cannot fake love you. My energy won't allow me to fake love anyone for longer than just a moment. I as well as you all do not have a poker face. We can only hold off so long before that lip flares, or eyes lock in. Pure, genuine, honest love. Go get some. Reciprocate it and live happily ever after, although this is not the end.

Now that we've re-aligned, I ask you... Why settle? We carefully choose every other aspect of our lives from the type of car we drive to the softness of the blankets we snuggle in at night... but somehow our REALationships constantly drain us. Why do we allow people to treat us poorly? Why don't we hold our friends, family and loved ones to a higher standard? Simply put, we're comfortable.

See the worst part about being comfortable, is that we're past complacency. To be comfortable is contented and undisturbed, undisturbed! To be complacent is the satisfaction of your own abilities or situation that you feel you do not need to try any harder.

Here is where the decision to settle is birthed. Do I step out of my comfort zone to potentially find a genuine love, or do I continue to go through the motions because I've been doing this for so long? Remember, time invested does NOT equal love. Nor does time invested equate to what you're required to put up with. Don't settle! Be open with your demands and communicate effectively. If you can drive across town because that restaurant is better than that other restaurant up the street from your house, you can make a careful decision on who to share your energy with.

"Love Me! Or Leave Me Alone." About as simple as it will get. But, don't forget that everybody loves differently. The way you express your love to me may differ in how I express my love to you. That's perfectly fine. It's so easy to get caught up in the details. Love isn't the details, because it's the unwritten paragraphs between the lines. The way I feel when my girl lights up when she sees me, unexplainable. I could talk to you until I'm blue and although you may understand what I'm telling you, you'll never feel me. I read a body of work about the languages of love. It really put a lot of things into perspective for me. Mainly, love is all about perspective. Having the ability to remove your own emotions and need for gratification opens you up to receive and provide love at a higher frequency. Love is all energy, and if you know like I know, energy cannot be created nor destroyed. If I love you, and I mean genuinely love you, that love will live forever, no matter what our relationship status is. So please, be sure to love and let love. Let love take over you and fill you up. Remember you must find your own happiness. Trust love and allow her to be your guide. She does not hurt, nor is she wrong. Please, please,

Love Me! Or Leave Me Alone!

SAUCE

Discipline, resistance...could've sworn I was a misfit.
Mama always told me, "baby, God made you different!"
Persistent, consistent, never failing to leave my imprint.
Small with the heart of a lion and I'm gifted.
Intellectual with a yearning desire to burn and get lifted.
I'm sorry, Tuck... is my name did I forget to mention?
Smoother than a pimp suit I hope you pay attention.
Convinced, bold, residing in my own dimension.
Resilient, brave, yet again he's in detention.
Damn not again, so much potential I hope he don't waste it.
Vulnerable to everything and consumed by the fakest.
Confused on the rules of the streets and who made them.
Lost in the sauce and only God could save them.
Decision making was shaky,
life flashed so many times so glad I was awakened.
Shout out to my Mama man she's the reason I'm free.
If it wasn't for her,
the world would've taken me.

RUFF LOVE

Dedicated to Bryson and Courtney Ruffin on their wedding day
June 1. 2019. Punta Cana, Dominican Republic

LOVE!

Thunderstorms in paradise
Marriage is the ultimate sacrifice
So many chances to get it wrong
Yet with you it's always right!

LOVE!

Is a gamble much more complex than rolling the dice.
You've went all in not once but twice.
Perfect harmony equals creation of life.
Today is the day a man looks beyond himself to
make this woman a wife.

LOVE!

Unity, dedication and peace!
In awe as we all watch him sweep her off of her feet.

LOVE!

With you, he is now complete!

TABLE FOR TWO PLEASE

Written by Rodney Tucker

Illustrated by Leeron Morraes

Edited by Tahlonna Grant

WWW.BEANSPROUTBOOKS.COM

Beansprout Books LLC | Morongo Valley, California

www.ingramcontent.com/pod-product-compliance
Lightning Source LLC
Chambersburg PA
CBHW030134100526
44591CB00009B/646